AF484682

Going on Safari!

A Read-Along Adventure

Spencer Mundree

Abbey Bryant

In a big white truck we started our tour

we were very excited
to begin to explore!

We drove near and far
for animals to see

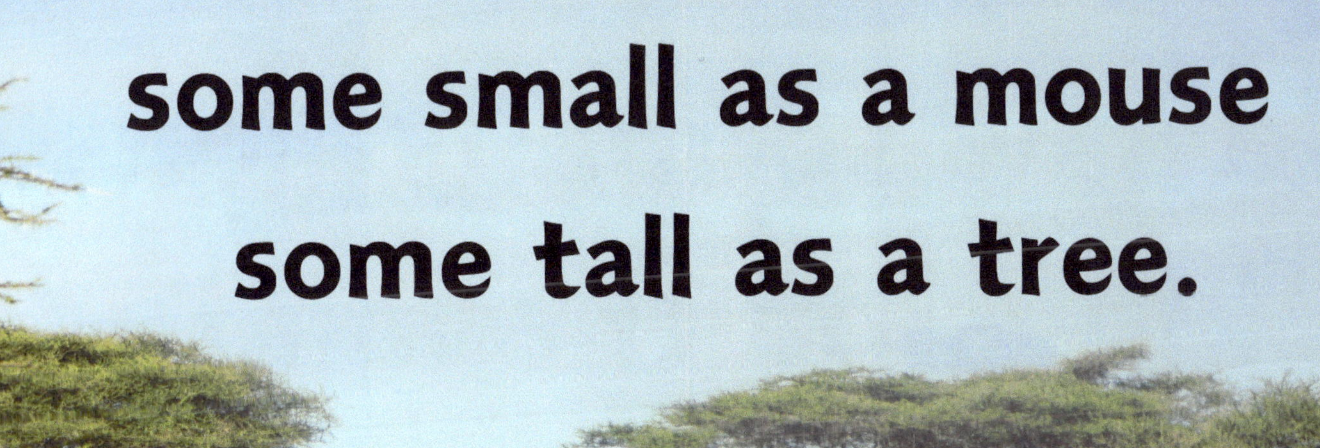

some small as a mouse
some tall as a tree.

We saw so many lions,
kings of the land,

and little lion cubs
the color of sand.

Big daddy lions with long flowing manes.

Mommy lions too,
searching the plains.

Migrating herds, of so many types

wildebeest, buffalos, and zebras

with stripes!

A big group of elephants, they're called a parade,

were all
very happy

eating trees
in the shade.

There were elephant babies, by mommy's side

trying to keep up with her HUMONGOUS stride!

We saw cheetahs run fast!
As fast as a car!

With black spotted fur,
you can see from afar.

Beautiful cheetahs,

so exciting to see

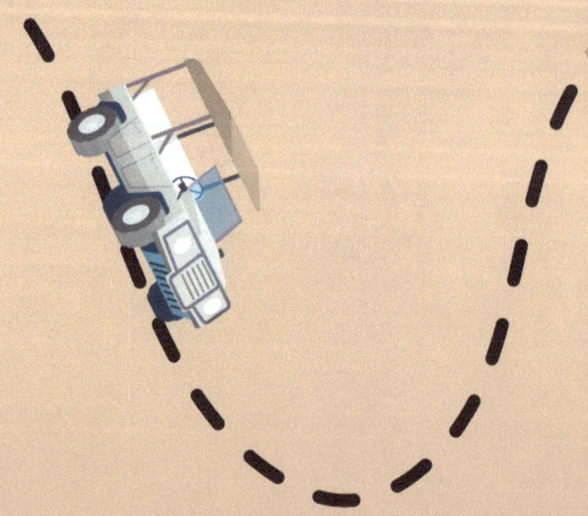

a mommy, her kids...
a family of 3!

Giraffes stretched up

high, with necks

oh so long, eating a lot,

to grow big and strong!

Picking their food, from the tiptops of trees,

no other animal can reach those tall leaves.

Birds were flying, monkeys were strolling

lions were yawning

laying and rolling.

Hippos were bathing

and buffalos grazing

Leopards in trees were truly amazing!

We

saw

ostriches

run,

lions

roar in

the sun

our safari adventure
was so much
FUN!

www.ingramcontent.com/pod-product-compliance
Lightning Source LLC
Chambersburg PA
CBHW042051100726
47973CB00014B/209